Every Day
with Je

for New
Christians

First Steps in the Christian Faith

Daily Devotional Readings for New Christians
by Selwyn Hughes

Revised and updated by Mick Brooks

Further Study section compiled by Trevor J. Partridge

Copyright © CWR, 1982, 2001, 2017.

Revised in 2001. Reprinted 2003 (twice), 2004, 2005 (twice), 2006, 2007, 2008, 2009, 2011, 2013, 2014, 2016.
This edition revised and reformatted 2017. Reprinted in 2019 (twice).

Cover picture: Adobe Stock/Melpomene
Concept development, editing, design and production by CWR.
Photographs: pixabay.com, fotosearch.com.
Printed in England by Bishops

Every Day with Jesus is available by subscription from CWR, Waverley Abbey House, Waverley Lane, Farnham, Surrey GU9 8EP, UK. Tel: (+44)1252 784700

All rights reserved, including serialisation and translation. No part of this publication may be reproduced, stored in a retrieval system, or transmitted, in any form or by any means, electronic, mechanical, photocopying, recording or otherwise, without the prior permission in writing of CWR.

For a list of National Distributors, visit cwr.org.uk/distributors

Unless otherwise indicated, all Scripture verses are taken from the Holy Bible, New International Version® Anglicised, NIV® Copyright © 1979, 1984, 2011 by Biblica, Inc.® Used by permission. All rights reserved worldwide.

Scripture marked TLB: The Living Bible copyright © 1971 by Tyndale House Foundation. Used by permission of Tyndale House Publishers Inc., Carol Stream, Illinois 60188. All rights reserved. The Living Bible, TLB, and the The Living Bible logo are registered trademarks of Tyndale House Publishers. *The Message*: Scripture taken from *The Message*. Copyright © 1993, 1994, 1995, 1996, 2000, 2001, 2002. Used by permission of NavPress Publishing Group. Moffatt: The Moffatt Translation of the Bible, © 1987, Hodder & Stoughton, New International Version: (NIV) Copyright © 1979, 1984 by Biblica (formerly International Bible Society). Used by permission of Hodder & Stoughton Publishers, an Hachette UK company.

CWR is a registered charity – No. 294387

CWR is a limited company registered in England – No. 1990308

How to get the best from this booklet

1. Come to each day's reading quietly

Try to find somewhere you are unlikely to be interrupted. Adopt an attitude that says, 'Speak, LORD, for your servant is listening' (1 Sam. 3:9).

2. Read the whole Bible passage

Turn over the passage in your mind and ask yourself: what is it really saying to me? Each part of the Bible is best understood in its context, so it's helpful to read the surrounding passage to see how it gives meaning to the text.

3. Read the notes carefully

Remember each day's comments are part of an overall theme. Try to remember what you read the previous day so that you maintain a sense of continuity. If there are words you do not understand, underline them and look them up in a dictionary, or ask a Christian friend to explain them to you. The 'Further Study' sections will help your understanding and personal development.

4. Think and pray

The prayer at the end of each study will hopefully capture the main thought of the day. As far as you can, try to identify yourself with the prayer. Feel free to add your own personal prayer to the one written. This will help you develop your own prayer life.

5. Share your discoveries

Find a Christian friend with whom you can talk over anything you discover in your reading that interests or intrigues you. What you share with others will cut a deeper path into your own life, and what is more it might be helpful to someone else.

How to look up a verse

1. Locate the book from the Contents page of your Bible.

2. Then locate the chapter (usually large type).

3. Then find the verse numbers (usually smaller and slightly raised).

John 3: 16–20

The Bible

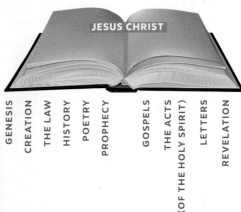

OLD TESTAMENT   NEW TESTAMENT

JESUS CHRIST

GENESIS
CREATION
THE LAW
HISTORY
POETRY
PROPHECY
GOSPELS
THE ACTS (OF THE HOLY SPIRIT)
LETTERS
REVELATION

<u>01</u> The goal

ROMANS 8:28–39

'from the very beginning God decided that those who came to him... should become like his Son' (v29, TLB)

We begin this special issue of *Every Day with Jesus* by looking at God's great purpose for our lives as His children. We'll explore together the different ways by which we can grow in our Christian lives in order to become all that God had originally planned for us to be. God's highest purpose for every Christian is seen in our opening verse. As you read it, allow it to sink deep down into your being. Just think of it! Before you ever appeared on this earth God knew all about you, and knew that the greatest thing He could ever achieve in your life was to help you live like His Son, Jesus Christ. And since you became a Christian, He's been on the case!

Through the problems

Romans 8:28 says, 'And we know that all that happens to us is working for our good if we love God and are fitting into his plans' (TLB). This highlights one of the ways in which God makes us more like Jesus. He uses everything that happens to us – difficulties, problems and other struggles – to develop our character and helps us be more like His Son. Through the disappointments and discouragements (as well as the joys and successes), God has been using everything to draw us to Himself.

Like Jesus

God wants you and me to live like Jesus! Think about that for a moment. God's highest purpose is not to make us missionaries, preachers, ministers, doctors or teachers – but to help us live like His Son. Everything else is secondary to this overall purpose. Given that this is God's highest aim for our lives, it is probably something worth thinking about! So ask yourself: 'Am I willing to make it a major focus of my life to live like Jesus? Am I prepared, with His help and strength, to live the way He wants me to? How can I become more like Him?'

PRAYER: Dear Lord Jesus, help me to become more like You. Let me have a new understanding of Your love and grace in my daily life, helping me to overcome every difficulty that prevents me from becoming like You. This I ask in Your precious name. Amen.

FOR FURTHER STUDY

Psalm 23:1–6; John 3:16; 2 Peter 1:3–4
1. How can we become more like Jesus?
2. How does He lead us?

---

02 What is a disciple?

JOHN 8:28–36

Jesus said, "If you hold to my teaching, you really are my disciples." (v31)

Throughout the Gospels (Matthew, Mark, Luke and John), one word is used more than any other to describe the relationship between Jesus and His followers.

That word is 'disciple'. The word means 'a trained one' or 'a learner'. Disciples are those who gather around a famous teacher and are trained by him in some special mission or task. As the students follow their teacher, learning from him and imitating him, they soon find themselves becoming like him in more ways than one. They begin to talk like him, walk like him and even think like him.

Jesus' school of discipleship

Let's make it our aim, during these readings, to sit at the feet of the greatest teacher of all time – Jesus – and learn so much of Him that we become like Him in every aspect of our lives. In this sense of wonder, let's approach Jesus and enter into His school of discipleship to learn more of Him through His Word.

One basic textbook

Today I am inviting you to enrol in this 'school of discipleship'. The teacher, if you like, is Jesus, and there is one basic textbook – the Bible. The more time you can spend in the Bible, the quicker you will grow in your faith. No one can be a true disciple of Jesus without spending some time regularly in His Word – Christians who grow in strength and purpose are those who spend time daily with God in His Word. Make it a priority to read a part of the Bible every day. Some days it might not always be possible, but as far as you are able, aim to spend some time each day with God in His Word.

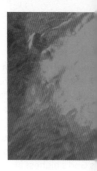

PRAYER: Heavenly Father, I see today that to become more like Your Son Jesus, I need to spend time reading Your Word. Please help me to do this every day. Amen.

FOR FURTHER STUDY
2 Timothy 2:1–15; John 8:12; Matthew 16:24
1. How can we learn more of God's truth?
2. What is the mark of a disciple?

<u>03</u> Counting the cost

LUKE 14:25–33
'first sit down and estimate the cost' (v28)

When Jesus was here upon the earth, He constantly challenged men and women with the call of discipleship. He didn't use emotional appeals to sweep people off their feet, but made it clear to them what it really meant to follow God. He does not say, 'Follow me, and you will never have to face discouragement or difficulty,' and nor does He say, 'Come with me, and you will never have another problem.' He outlines His offer in straight-talking terms, and this is why He refers to the illustration of a man about to build a tower who first sits down to count the cost.

Jesus wants relationship

Have you ever counted the cost of being a disciple of Jesus? Let's see if we can consider His call together. He longs for real relationship – and He's paid the price on the cross, that we might live and walk with Him as He originally designed. He wants to partner with us throughout the rest of our lives.

'Blood, sweat, toil and tears'

Why does He ask this of us? Because, like the man who built the tower, Jesus, too, is in the world to build a kingdom. It isn't a kingdom made of wood or stone, but a kingdom of love, in the hearts of His people. To build that kingdom He needs men and women, both young and old, who will follow Him fully, freely and unconditionally.

In his first speech to the British Parliament in World War II, Winston Churchill offered the nation nothing but 'blood, sweat, toil and tears'. Are you willing to offer Jesus your love, your loyalty and your whole life – today?

PRAYER: Yes, Lord Jesus, my life is Yours to take and use as You see fit. I want to be a true disciple of Yours, both today and every day of my life. Amen.

FOR FURTHER STUDY
Matthew 19:16–30; Galatians 5:24;
1 Timothy 6:17–19
1. Why was the young man sorrowful?
2. What did Jesus promise the disciples?

04 Don't look back

LUKE 9:57–62

'No procrastination. No backward looks.
You can't put God's kingdom off till
tomorrow. Seize the day.'
(v62, *The Message*)

You can be sure that as you decide to
commit yourself to Jesus, many things
will come before you that may try to
distract you from the deep commitment
you have made. I would not be surprised
if already a number of things have
happened to you that have challenged
your faith. But don't worry about that,
for as you grapple with challenges, so
you will grow.

The call to full surrender

In today's reading we see three men
who each felt drawn to follow Jesus,
but allowed something to come
between them and the call to follow
Him. The first man volunteered to follow
Jesus anywhere He went, but when
told that Jesus had nowhere to sleep,
we hear no more of him. The second
man was called by Jesus to special
service, but there was something else
he felt he ought to do before taking that
step. The third man offered his life to
Christ, but insisted that he should first
be allowed to say goodbye to his family.

Putting Jesus first

Let's be clear that Jesus does not expect
us to ignore our families, or turn our
back on responsibility – but if it comes
to a test, then He wants to be first
on the scale of our priorities. We are
living at a time when the great call to
follow Jesus is sometimes up against
problems that no prior generation has
had to face. God longs for us to shine
as lights in an age that is getting darker
and darker. Having 'put your hand to
the plough', don't look back, but keep
your eyes fixed firmly on your master,
who stands out in front. Make Him your
highest priority, and make up your mind
that whatever happens, you will follow
through with Jesus in every possible way.

PRAYER: Having found You as my Saviour and Lord, I can see that there is nothing I can ever compare with You. Lord Jesus, You are the captain of my salvation and the Saviour of my soul. Amen.

FOR FURTHER STUDY

Matthew 6:19–34; Luke 12:7; 1 Peter 5:7

1. What is God's promise to those who follow Him?
2. How did Jesus illustrate this?

05 Cleaning up

1 JOHN 1:1–10

'If we confess our sins, he is faithful and just and will forgive us our sins and purify us from all unrighteousness.' (v9)

One of the greatest discoveries we can make in living a fruitful Christian life is this: God's strength will flow into our lives when we learn how to confess our sins and receive from Him His complete forgiveness.

Immediate confession

God forgave all our sins at the time of our conversion, but because we live day by day in a fallen world, we sometimes forget our commitment to follow Jesus, and fall into personal sin of one form or another. Whether we lie, steal, cheat, swear, blaspheme or lose our temper, immediately our hearts become aware that we've let God down and sin has entered our lives. What should we do on such occasions? Well, if we simply grieve over the fact that we have sinned and take no further steps to correct the situation, we will become sad, discouraged and disappointed. The Bible's solution is immediate confession. That is, we should tidy up behind us – firstly by asking God to forgive us, then by asking those whom we have hurt or injured for their forgiveness too. When this is put into practice and kept to, then the Christian life becomes a pathway of power and peace. Our lives have been redeemed by the blood of Jesus, and there is no other way in which sin can be dealt with except by His forgiving love.

Christ forgives

Sin leaves marks, and our actions almost always affect other people – there will often be consequences for our sin. But when we call these things out before God and accept His forgiveness, there's nothing we can do that's too sinful for His love. We won't always be saved from consequences, but we will be forgiven, and God promises to walk with us through those consequences.

PRAYER: Father, how glad I am that despite my failings and sins, there is forgiveness to be found in You. Help me learn to confess my sins so that they will not hurt You, or any others I have injured. This I ask in Jesus' name. Amen.

FOR FURTHER STUDY
1 John 2:1–12; Ephesians 1:7; Psalm 130:4
1. What is an advocate?
2. How does this apply to us as Christians?

06 Your full weight

PSALM 55:1–23
'Cast your cares on the LORD and he will sustain you; he will never let the righteous be shaken.' (v22)

A missionary, when speaking to a group of Africans, needed an illustration to bring home to them the importance of trusting God completely. Out of the corner of his eye, in the distance, he could see a young African climbing a tree in order to pick the valued fruit. Pointing to this scene, the missionary preached a sermon that went something like this:

'If this young man climbs the tree by strength alone, then when he gets to the top he will be exhausted. Notice how he has woven the strands of a vine to form a strong rope, which fits around him and helps him as he climbs. As he leans his weight against the rope, he can climb the tree in safety, gather the fruit, and come back down without being exhausted. He can only do this as he remembers to lean his full weight back on the rope.'

Trusting God

Whatever load we have to carry for God must always be balanced by the energy, grace and strength of Jesus Himself. We can learn, in our work and witness, to shift the burden on to His broad shoulders. The Christian life is not a grim, determined fight in which we summon all our physical resources, but a life in which we learn to let God take the strain.

All our burdens

Some Christians who have not yet learned this lesson, might go through life struggling and striving, falling into bed at night on the point of exhaustion. Although God has an important part for you to play in serving Him, remember that, as we read in today's verse, He wants you to give Him all your burdens, for He has promised that He will carry them.

PRAYER: Thank You, dear Father, for showing me how to live the Christian life. Help me to lean on You with all my weight – and as I rely on You, I know You will never permit me to slip or fall. Amen.

FOR FURTHER STUDY
Isaiah 53; 40:28–31; Psalm 46:1; Nehemiah 8:10
1. What happens when we wait on the Lord?
2. What is our strength?

Learning to forgive

MATTHEW 6:5–15
'For if you forgive other people when they sin against you, your heavenly Father will also forgive you. But if you do not forgive others their sins, your Father will not forgive your sins.' (vv14–15)

Someone once said to John Wesley, 'I'll never forgive anyone.' 'Then I hope, sir,' said Wesley, 'that you never sin.' You see, today's Bible verse clearly shows us that forgiving and being forgiven are all of a piece. If we want forgiveness, we must forgive. Don't go through life bearing resentments, because these will eat into you and infect your whole being. Any doctor will tell you that a person who bears resentment, or refuses to forgive, will end up a sick person. You see, we are not made by God to carry bitterness, and when we do, it imposes a load upon us that we are not able to bear.

Harbouring resentment

I knew a man in South Wales many years ago who never felt that he was truly 'saved'. He had repented of his sin, joined a church, and attended all the services, but still felt no real spiritual assurance. One day a counsellor asked him if he was holding resentment against anyone, and he confessed that he had a strong bitterness towards a man who had cheated him out of a small fortune many years earlier. The counsellor suggested that he needed to get the bitterness out of his heart, and after confessing it and letting it go into God's hands, the man no longer had any difficulties with the problem of assurance. He knew he was saved; he had no doubts about it.

Forgiving others

What had happened? As he forgave the other man, then God's forgiveness flooded into his own heart, bringing a sustaining strength and assurance with it. God's forgiveness was there before, but the man was unable to receive it into his heart because of the blockage caused by his own bitterness. When we forgive others, then God's forgiveness is able to reach into every area of our being.

PRAYER: Lord, I don't want to go through life with bitterness and resentment in my heart against anyone. Teach me how to be a forgiving person. In Jesus' name. Amen.

FOR FURTHER STUDY
Matthew 18:21–35; Mark 11:25; Ephesians 4:32
1. What did Jesus teach in the above parable?
2. How many times should we forgive?

Forgive yourself

2 CORINTHIANS 2:1–11
'I also forgive.' (v10)

There are many people in the family of God who don't doubt God's forgiveness, but they never seem able to forgive themselves. The memory of their sin lacerates them. Far from being able, as some are, to forgive themselves easily, they seem unable to forgive themselves at all. Just like an unhealed wound in the body, this unhealed wound

in the spirit hinders their progress, allows infection into the bloodstream, and keeps them in a state of spiritual paralysis. There must be literally millions of Christians who have never properly understood this truth: God has forgiven you – so forgive yourself.

Spiritual pride

Unwillingness to forgive yourself could be a form of spiritual pride. What you might really be saying is: 'How could I ever have done that?' But that self-hate will do you no good. It stirs the self-destructive principle in your nature, like a poison injected into your veins. Accept God's forgiveness, and forgive yourself, for if God has forgiven, who can justly accuse? Let these words sink deep into your spirit today: 'Who dares accuse us whom God has chosen...? Will God? No! He is the one who has forgiven us... Who then will condemn us? Will Christ? *No!* For he is the one who died for us... nothing will ever be able to separate us from the love of God' (Rom. 8:33–34,38, TLB).

God's tenderness

The other thing to learn is this: when you give your sin to God, He uses it. Not by encouraging you to talk about it, but rather to use it as a driving force in your will, to quicken your compassion for others, and to show God's tenderness to the fallen when other Christians might just give the impression that God is hard and unforgiving.

PRAYER: I thank You, Lord, that You have forgiven all my sin. Help me now to forgive myself, and to lay down my pride at Your feet. Amen.

FOR FURTHER STUDY
1 John 1; Proverbs 18:14; Ephesians 1:6; Colossians 2:10
1. What happens when we walk in God's light?
2. How can a wounded spirit be healed?

09 Taking up the cross

MATTHEW 16:13–28
'Then Jesus said to his disciples, "Whoever wants to be my disciple must deny themselves and take up their cross and follow me."' (v24)

The phrase 'take up your cross' can sometimes be puzzling to someone new to faith, so let me explain what the term really means. In the days in which Jesus lived, a cross meant just one thing – death. Whenever a cross was uplifted, it meant that someone had to die in the most horrible way imaginable – in the agony of crucifixion.

Be known as a Christian

Of course, 'taking up our cross' does not mean that we nail two pieces of wood together and carry it around on our backs as a sign that we are followers of Jesus. It simply means that we become willing to 'die' to our own selfishness and self-centredness. Let's take a specific example. To be known as a Christian may make you unpopular with colleagues at work. They may laugh at the name of Jesus. It is not easy to stand against this kind of talk, and our own human nature will tend to speak to us deep within and say: 'Don't tell anyone you follow Jesus...' Taking up your cross would be to deny your own desire for the approval of others, and willingly bear their mocking for the sake of Jesus.

Put Jesus first

It is important to remember, of course, that whenever you make up your mind to put Jesus first and your own desires second, a special supply of grace is directed towards you by God. It will not be as tough as you think, for God's help is given to all those who step out to obey Him and live life His way. If you decide to 'take up your cross', I promise you an amazing new discovery – by denying self and putting God first, you will know the joy of becoming more like Jesus.

PRAYER: Dear Lord Jesus, I do so long to be strong and bold in my testimony for You. Help me to accept this challenge, and to deny my own selfish pleasure, so that You can be glorified in me this very day. Amen.

FOR FURTHER STUDY
Romans 6; Galatians 2:20; 6:14–15
1. Who wrote Romans and Galatians?
2. How did Paul live his new life?

Growing in holiness

1 PETER 1:13–2:3
'But just as he who called you is holy,
so be holy in all you do' (1:15)

Peter's call to us to 'be holy' may, to some people, seem either frightening or impossible, so let's see if we can bring it a little more into focus.

Becoming holy

How do we become holy? Well, the way we can become holy is to become more like Jesus Christ, and the highest goal we can ever have, as we have been seeing, is to become like Him in every way possible. Becoming holy is a process that unfolds as we take more and more of Jesus into our lives each day. You see, we generally invite Jesus into a few areas of our lives, or into one area at a time. I know of no one who has allowed Jesus to come into every area of their life all at once. I certainly didn't. I committed myself to Christ the day I got saved. After that, as I attended church and read His Word day by day, I realised that there were more and more areas of my life that had to come under His influence. One by one I gave them to Him. Sometimes I struggled to keep some areas for myself, but His love was so gracious as He kept bringing me back time and time again to the challenge I needed to accept.

Surrender

Perhaps this is what He is doing with you now. Does God seem to bring you back time and time again to the same question? Does He speak to you in a sermon, in a book or in the words of a friend, about one issue in particular? Then it's because He wants that area committed to Him. Every compartment of your life will, when given over to Him, become perfected by His presence and indwelling. Are there some parts of your personality that have not yet been 'cleaned up' by Christ? Don't keep Him out of any area into which He wants to come: surrender all to Him this day.

PRAYER: Dear Father, I am so sorry that I struggle to keep my own independence, and keep You out of those parts of my life that really would be better with You. Help me this day to surrender in a deeper way than ever before. In Jesus' name. Amen.

FOR FURTHER STUDY
1 Timothy 4; Hebrews 12:14;
2 Corinthians 3:18; Psalm 92:12
1. What did Paul encourage Timothy to do?
2. What are the godly likened to?

Every disciple an ambassador

2 CORINTHIANS 5:14–21
'We are therefore Christ's ambassadors'
(v20)

Every disciple of Jesus is called to be an ambassador. An ambassador is someone who represents his king in a foreign land, and the task of sharing Jesus with those with whom you come in contact day by day is all part of your task as Christ's ambassador. Your King is in heaven, but He has a great interest in all people on this earth.

Daily contact

An ambassador has certain responsibilities to undertake for king and country. One of them is to convey the wishes of his king to those with whom he lives. For this reason, any correspondence that comes from a monarch to his or her ambassador anywhere in the world is protected by special rights. All messages are secure, encrypted and protected, and arrive at the 'desk' of the ambassador totally uncompromised. In this way, the ambassador is kept in weekly (if not daily) contact with 'king and country'.

Messages every day

Something similar happens to those of us who belong to Jesus and take our place in this world as His ambassadors. We too have daily dispatches – when we open the Bible each day, we are actually reading the message of our heavenly King to our hearts. Today, as you read these lines, this is what is happening to you.

Your King – the Lord Jesus Christ – is speaking direct to your heart through His Word, the Bible. He is reminding you of the joy of being His ambassador. As you go out today to face the world, remember your high calling. You are an ambassador of the King of kings. He has given you letters (the Bible), which are His special instructions for your life. Talk to someone today about your great King.

PRAYER: Father, how brilliant a responsibility You have given me to share Your love with a lost world. Help me to be a faithful ambassador, and create an opportunity for me today to share Your love with someone. Amen.

FOR FURTHER STUDY
Acts 1:1–11; John 20:21; 2 Corinthians 3:2–3; 1 Peter 3:15
1. What did Jesus promise before He ascended?
2. What would this make the disciples?

<u>12</u> Disciples act as salt

LUKE 14:34–15:10
What good is salt that has lost its saltiness? Flavorless salt is fit for nothing' (vv34–35, TLB)

This verse is one of the most fascinating statements in the Bible, and follows on closely after Jesus has been defining the conditions of Christian discipleship.

Impurities

In the days of Jesus, salt, of course, was not found in the form we know it today. Two thousand years ago, people knew little about the purification process,

and so the salt often contained impurities such as sand, dirt and grime. Salt that was very impure was often thrown out or, because of its hard, rock-like quality, was put in the foundations of footpaths (take a look at Matthew 5:13). We can see at once from this that if our lives are full of impurities, then we shall not live as God wants us to live. We will become tasteless salt, fit only to be trodden underfoot.

As Christ's disciples, we are to be like salt in the world: pure, clean and wholesome. What are the things that cause our salt to lose its taste? Lying could be one. When we fail to face up to the truth in every way, this robs us of being effective disciples of Jesus. Anger could be another – the bitterness we show when asked to do something that we know must be done but tends to be time-consuming, boring or tiring.

Make others thirsty

One of the characteristics of salt we ought to bear in mind is that salt creates thirst. Eat some salt, and you will soon need to rush to the tap for a drink of water. If only today we could make others thirsty to know and understand the ways and character of God. May He grant that it may be so in each of our lives.

PRAYER: Lord, I want to be as salt to all those I meet this day, creating in them, through my love for You, a desire to know You as wonderfully as I do. This I ask in Jesus' name. Amen.

FOR FURTHER STUDY
Matthew 5:1–16; 1 Timothy 1:5; Psalm 24:3–4
1. What is another characteristic of salt?
2. What else does Jesus say we are to be like?

Morning prayer

PSALM 5:1–12
'In the morning, LORD, you hear my voice;
in the morning I lay my requests before
you and wait expectantly.' (v3)

No one can ever hope to live a Christian life without constant attention to prayer. We grow in Christ according to the time we give to communion with God in private prayer. All the saints down the ages who have achieved great service for God have said that it came primarily through prayer.

A simple plan

Here's a simple plan that can help you begin your day with God, and add richness and meaning to your daily experience with Him. As soon as you open your eyes in the morning, learn to greet the day with a simple, 'Thank You, Jesus.' Then, as soon as possible after awakening, try to fence off some time – say, 15 minutes – just for you and Jesus to be together. In the first five minutes, read a portion of the Bible so that your mind begins to focus on the Word of God. You can either use what is set out in these daily notes or a passage you have chosen yourself, but do read the Bible – it will freshen your mind and bring your thoughts into line with God's.

Praying to God

Then, spend the next five minutes in simple meditation, thinking about the piece of Scripture you have read, and asking yourself if there is any challenge it has brought to your life that ought to be taken up. In this period, share with God any issues, struggles and hopes. Tell Him your secret fears and troubles. Then, in the final five minutes, remember to turn your prayers outward on behalf of others – your friends who don't yet know Jesus, your work colleagues, your family.

Finally, praise the Lord! Give Him thanks, and remember that He is with you, in you and for you. Now, have a good day!

PRAYER: Lord, help me to develop a daily habit of beginning each morning in Your presence. Teach me patience, love and obedience, that I may receive all You have to give me this day. Amen.

FOR FURTHER STUDY
Luke 11:1–3; Isaiah 65:24; John 15:7
1. What does God promise when we pray?
2. Write down some people and things to pray about.

Evening prayer

PSALM 92

'Every morning tell him, "Thank you for your kindness," and every evening rejoice in all his faithfulness.' (v2, TLB)

Some Christians believe that a few minutes of early morning prayer is all that is needed to build an effective Christian life, but those who really aim to follow Jesus will, like the disciples of old, find time to come to Him in the evening also.

Review the day

How can we get the best out of the moments we spend with God at the end of the day? Find some time (I'd suggest a minimum of ten minutes) towards the close of the day and get alone with God in private prayer. Review the day in God's presence. Think over the moments of weakness and bring them to Jesus for forgiveness. There will no doubt be cause for thanksgiving as you recollect the goodness of God in your life. Spend a few minutes thanking Him for all the small things in life and for who He is! There will be things, of course, that will come before you with some degree of urgency, such as a friend who is desperately sick, or someone in your family who is in great need. Pray for them by name, asking God to heal and minister to them by His own divine power.

Before you sleep

Your last thoughts before you fall asleep can be of God and His goodness. Sink into the thought of God's love even more deeply than you sink into your bed. Rest your whole weight upon Him. The mind continues to work in remarkable ways even when we are asleep, and you will be amazed at how, when you give your mind spiritual thoughts to dwell on, they will infiltrate the deepest parts of your being during the night hours. I find it's often helpful to choose a portion of the Bible to reflect on just before falling asleep. You will find that filling your mind with thoughts of God and His love will provide the best possible rest, and will be the greatest tonic for tomorrow.

PRAYER: Dear Lord, I am learning day by day the importance of my daily communion with You. Help me to grow, moment by moment, into all that You want me to be. Amen.

FOR FURTHER STUDY

Psalm 119:9–16; 63:6; Philippians 4:8; Isaiah 26:3

1. Where had the psalmist put God's Word?
2. What things should we think about?

PSALM 107:1–22

'Oh, that these men would praise the Lord for his loving-kindness, and for all of his wonderful deeds!' **(v8, TLB)**

Someone has said that there are two types of Christian in the world – those who take things for granted, and those who take things with gratitude. Which kind are you? What does your attitude tend to be like in the morning, regardless of tiredness, circumstances or weather? Let's learn to thank God for all the things we do have, rather than worrying about the things we don't.

Praise God

The encouragement of the psalmist in this psalm, and in many others, is to give thanks to God continually for all the blessings of life. When we are true disciples of Jesus, we will always recognise the importance of this truth. Without praise, our lives are empty, and we can never enjoy to its fullest extent the life God has planned for us. The New Testament also reminds us of this important responsibility in these words: 'Always give thanks for everything to our God and Father in the name of our Lord Jesus Christ' (Eph. 5:20, TLB).

Start now

Start today by taking every opportunity to praise God. Begin by thanking Him for the sleep that you enjoyed last night, and the roof over your head, and the last meal you ate. Then thank Him for the challenge of a new day. Go on through the day looking for things for which you can praise Him! And if you can't find any, then praise Him for His Son, the Lord Jesus Christ, and for His marvellous salvation, purchased for you on the cross of Calvary. There is no end to the things for which you can praise Him – there's no reason not to start now!

PRAYER: Father God, forgive me for often being slow to praise You when all around me I see so much of Your love and care. Help me overcome this indifference so that I might continually glorify Your name. Amen.

FOR FURTHER STUDY

Psalm 150:1–6; Philippians 4:4–6;
1 Thessalonians 5:16–18
1. How are we to praise the Lord?
2. For what should we give thanks?

16 The art of listening

1 SAMUEL 3:1–10
'The LORD came and stood there, calling as at the other times, "Samuel! Samuel!" Then Samuel said, "Speak, for your servant is listening."' (v10)

There are two sides to prayer – one is talking to God, the other is letting God talk to you. Having talked with hundreds of Christians at different times, I have discovered that most have yet to master the art of listening to God while in prayer. Let's see if we can understand something of the art of listening today.

Listen to God

When you have finished talking to God in your prayer time today, don't immediately rush off about your business, but spend five minutes waiting quietly before Him, listening to His voice. Many people fill every moment of their prayer time by talking non-stop to God. No real relationship will flourish under such circumstances – conversation is rarely one-sided! Common courtesy requires, at any time, that we listen as well as speak. At first, all you will hear is your own thoughts, or the traffic in the distance or other distracting sounds, but gradually, as you practise this, you will begin to hear God speak to you in words that are unmistakable and clear.

His voice will become familiar

How does a morse code operator learn to understand the messages that come through his radio set? By practising – and the more time you spend before God quietly listening for His voice, the sooner the time will come when it will become so familiar that you will instantly recognise Him the moment He begins speaking to you. God's voice may not always be strong and clear. The closeness of your walk with God will determine that. But I promise you that if you take the time to listen, God will take the time to talk with you.

PRAYER: Yes, Lord, I will be that one – teach me how to be quiet and to wait before You, so that I might hear Your voice and listen to Your message to my heart. This I ask in Jesus' name. Amen.

FOR FURTHER STUDY
Isaiah 6:1–9; John 10:4; 1 Kings 19:12
1. In what sort of voice does God speak to us?
2. How did Isaiah respond to God's voice?

17 Following God's guidance

PSALM 31:1–24
'Since you are my rock and my fortress, for the sake of your name lead and guide me.' (v3)

When we are listening for God's voice, we will respond to Him leading and guiding us. And Satan hates a guided Christian! He finds it difficult to trap or trip one who knows the way Jesus is leading; and much of the joy of successful Christian living lies right here.

God guides in many ways:

1. Through His Word. Sometimes, as you read the Bible, a particular verse will stand out. Be careful about this, though, as many have been misled by taking a verse out of context and assuming it to be divine guidance. Usually prayer and waiting upon God will either confirm or contradict whatever arises from your daily reading.

2. Through our reason. As we wait before God in prayer, and His truth resonates in our soul, we begin to think the thoughts of God and catch the amazing discovery of His will.

3. Through circumstances. Sometimes doors close and other doors mysteriously open. We pick up a magazine or a letter, seemingly by chance, and our lives are altered by something we see. I have always found it a safe rule to stay in one sphere of service until God opens another more effective, wider and more important door. If a door closes, thank God for it. There will be another one opening up shortly.

The listening side of prayer

Christians who have learned to pray but not to listen will find it difficult to get guidance. As we have said before, we often treat God in the way we treat our friends, and do all the talking! We give Him no time to talk to us, to whisper His confirmation or His word of change. To get guidance, let's not neglect the listening side of prayer. Tell Him your issues, then sit back and listen for the answer. It will come in a quiet, deliberate witness to your heart. Don't be anxious or too eager. Let all haste and tension go. As you sense His nearness, lay the issue before Him. Then go the way of peace.

PRAYER: Father, I need so much to learn the art of listening. Quieten my heart today that I might learn to listen for Your still small voice. In Jesus' name. Amen.

FOR FURTHER STUDY
Psalm 23:1–6; 48:14; Proverbs 3:5–6; Isaiah 42:16
1. To what is the Lord likened?
2. How has He promised to lead us?

¹⁸ Take a firm stand

EPHESIANS 6:10–20
'Stand firm then, with the belt of truth
buckled round your waist' (v14)

Sometimes people tell me that being
the only Christian in their school,
college or place of work can be pretty
tough. 'It's not easy to stand alone,'
they say, 'and I wonder whether I can
go on much longer.' It's surprising,
though, how many times I have talked
to Christians who have told me that they
came to Jesus because of the firm stand
that another person took as the only
Christian in their environment.

Make a stand for Christ

In my teens, when I first became a
Christian, I was the only Christian
among around a hundred men in the
engineering shop where I worked. It
was hard to tell them I had become a
Christian, but many of them told me
years later that my stand for Jesus
had made them more interested in the
message of the gospel, and some of
them became Christians because of it.

Wishbones instead of backbones

You see, when you nail your colours to
the mast as a disciple of Jesus, God will
use your witness in a most amazing way.
It may not look as if much is coming out
of it, but be sure that by standing firm
in your principles of loyalty to Jesus,
God will use it for His glory. Below the
surface, everyone admires someone
who has the courage to stand for
what they believe, and no one really

likes a coward. There are far too many people who have wishbones instead of backbones, and haven't the moral courage to stand for anything. Stand firm for the right things, even though you might be labelled, typecast and stereotyped. A word of caution – the devil will fight you all he can, and try to make you live in fear and believe things that aren't true. However, God will encourage you in a wonderful way – and remember, He is no farther away than the beat of your own heart.

PRAYER: Forgive me, dear Lord, for the times when I have been afraid to stand for the truth. Now that You have spoken to me like this, I am going to draw on Your strength day by day and take my stand firmly for You. In Jesus' name. Amen.

FOR FURTHER STUDY
Acts 13:42–52; 5:41; Matthew 5:11–16; 2 Timothy 3:12
1. What happened when Paul preached?
2. What are we to do when persecuted?

19 Ready for battle

2 TIMOTHY 2:1–13
'Join with me in suffering, like a good soldier of Christ Jesus.' (v3)

Paul is writing here to his good friend Timothy, and in encouraging him to push on and follow Jesus, he uses four different word pictures. First, he refers to him as a 'son' (v1), then a 'soldier' (v3); next, an 'athlete' or sportsman (v5), and finally a 'farmer' or sower (v6). As followers of Jesus, we are to be sons and daughters, soldiers, athletes and sowers, but the one particular picture I want to look at with you today is that of a soldier.

A spiritual battle
Christians are involved in a battle. There are two orders and two kingdoms in this world – the kingdom of God, and the kingdom of Satan. As we become Christians we are involved in a spiritual battle, in which Satan constantly seeks to gain the advantage over us. We are truly 'Christian soldiers' engaged in a fight against sin and Satan.

Some time ago I was in Israel, and during a conversation with a group of young people, I learned that every teenager is obliged to spend some time in the Israeli army. The political situation in the Middle East is so unsettled that war could come at any time, and every person, young and old, must be on the alert, trained and ready to take their place whenever and wherever they are needed.

Be on the alert
In our struggle against sin, our enemy, the devil, is constantly looking for ways in which he can launch an offensive against us and claim back some territory

for himself. As sons and daughters of the King of king's we are to be constantly on the alert, and ready to take a stand at any moment. Perhaps even today you might find yourself caught up in a situation that demands bravery and courage for your King. Remember – when standing with Jesus, you will always be on the winning side!

PRAYER: Father, I am proud to serve in Your great army. Help me to realise that I am in a war against sin and Satan, and strengthen me to be a good soldier of the Lord Jesus Christ. I ask this in Christ's precious name. Amen.

FOR FURTHER STUDY
Ephesians 6:10–18; 2 Corinthians 10:4; 1 Timothy 1:18
1. List the items of our spiritual armour.
2. What weapon has been given to us?

---

20 It takes courage

LUKE 9:23–26
'For whoever wants to save their life will lose it, but whoever loses their life for me will save it.' (v24)

We've already looked at what it means to 'take up our cross' as followers of Jesus, but I want us to revisit this idea of self-denial again today. The truth contained in this particular portion of the New Testament is really the foundation on which the truth of Christian discipleship is built.

Self-denial
Self-denial means going without some things that you like having, or doing things that you do not normally like doing. True disciples are always ready to take up the challenge of Jesus in this vital matter. What does it mean in terms of real practical examples? It may mean we have to be ready to give our testimony to a group of people who have asked us to do it – even when the prospect of speaking in public terrifies us. It may mean we have to think of the interests of others. It means that we make an effort to attend church, whether we feel like it or not.

Fair weather Christians
This is the kind of challenge Jesus presents to all those who want to be truly His, and this is why so many turn back from following Him. There are many who start off in the Christian life with a deep desire to commit themselves to Christ, but when the time of testing or challenge comes, they are not prepared to stand up and be counted. How strong is your commitment? Are you a 'fair weather Christian' – someone who practises the principles of Christ only when there is no real test or challenge?

Remember – God not only lifts the standard to what may seem unbelievable heights, He also provides the strength (the Holy Spirit) by which we can achieve them.

PRAYER: How glad I am, Lord, that You not only challenge me to live a meaningful Christian life, but when I surrender to You, I can experience the strengthening presence of the Holy Spirit, enabling me to live as You want me to live. Thank You, Father. Amen.

FOR FURTHER STUDY

Luke 14:16–35; 5:27–28; Romans 15:1
1. Why didn't the people attend the supper?
2. What did Jesus ask for from His followers?

21 Setting clear goals

PHILIPPIANS 3:4–14

'I press on towards the goal to win the prize for which God has called me heavenwards in Christ Jesus.' (v14)

The apostle Paul is comparing the Christian life here to a race in which all the contestants run towards a chosen mark or goal. Paul explains that, although he has been running the race of the Christian life for many years, he has still not arrived at his goal – so he keeps on running! What was Paul's goal? Jesus. Paul wanted to become more and more like Him in every way. As we have seen, this is the ultimate goal of every disciple of Christ – to become more and more like Jesus in every possible way.

Mentally

It might be a good time to pause for a moment and ask yourself: where am I in the race, and do I need to pick up the pace? What are the kind of goals I need to be aiming at to achieve this? We can do this by putting on the mind of Christ. How, you might say, can I have Christ's mind in me? Well, give your mind to Him, and He will give His mind to you. The more you think about Him, concentrate on Him and read His Word, the more your mind will become like His.

Spiritually

We can also aim to be like Jesus spiritually. That is, our spirits (the part of our being in which our conscience is situated) should be cultivated towards Christlikeness by prayer, daily Bible reading and instant confession whenever we make mistakes. Discipleship is not just giving half a life or half your heart, but giving the best you have for the best God has for you.

PRAYER: Yes, dear Lord, I want You to have the best I have to give, since I know You have given Your best for me. Amen.

FOR FURTHER STUDY

Philippians 2:1–13; 1 Corinthians 6:19; John 1:14

1. As Christians, what have our bodies become?
2. List some characteristics of Jesus.

Keep at it

1 CORINTHIANS 15:51–58

'be strong and steady, always abounding in the Lord's work, for you know that nothing you do for the Lord is ever wasted' (v58, TLB)

Once, while in Haiti, I stopped at a little shop to buy a present for my wife. On one of the counters I saw a whole army of little figures carved out of wood. I was impressed by the hours of work that must have gone into them, and I asked the shop owner, 'How ever did you do it?' He smiled and said, 'I just kept at it.' I have a friend in South Wales who used the same phrase. His house and garden were beautifully kept, but

before he began working on it, it had been a complete mess – it was just a wilderness. When I asked him how he had achieved so much, he gave me the same reply: 'I just kept at it.'

Overcoming

Let's allow the same spirit to grip us – a 'keeping on'. It shows up in all the Bible characters who lived fruitful lives for God. They kept at it. The apostle Paul continually urges his readership to persevere in their faith. Whatever trials we may face, we are to press on, drawing ever closer to Jesus and trusting in His ways. It is by His strength that we can overcome any obstacle. When we are tempted to give up, we can remind ourselves of Paul's words: 'nothing you do for the Lord is ever wasted' (v58).

Good endings

A great many good but ineffective people concentrate on their beginnings but not their endings – they lose sight of the finish line. They take up things but don't carry them through. In 1 Corinthians 16:8–9, Paul said there were many things to thwart him but he kept to the task. 'I am staying on... I have wide opportunities here' (Moffatt). Many of us might have said, 'There are many problems so I'm quitting.' This is why Paul became such a great apostle. He kept at it!

PRAYER: Lord, I feel like shouting it from the rooftops – with You in my life, I can overcome all the obstacles which are against me. Thank You, Father! Amen.

FOR FURTHER STUDY
Luke 18:1–8; Galatians 5:1; Philippians 1:27
1. Why did the judge grant the woman's request?
2. What is the reward for persistence?

23 No despair

2 CORINTHIANS 4:1–14

'We are hard pressed on every side, but not crushed; perplexed, but not in despair' (v8)

The apostle Paul was, without doubt, one of the greatest examples of true discipleship to be found anywhere in the New Testament, and he consistently encourages us to continue 'running the race' for Christ. In the list of difficulties outlined in today's passage, he is not seeking sympathy, but explaining how to deal with such things. Paul recognised that because of his relationship to Jesus Christ, God would never allow any situation to come his way unless it could further God's purposes and interests.

For our good

Now that's a fascinating thought, isn't it? If God will not allow anything to overtake us unless it can work to His and our good, then we can face our problems with a spirit of optimism rather than hopelessness. This truth is perhaps one of the most life-changing revelations of the New Testament. What could we discover more meaningful than the fact that God will never allow anything to happen to one of His children unless He foresees that He can ultimately work it out for good in that person's life? This is why Paul could say, 'We get knocked down, but we get up again and keep going.'

The greatest message

Whatever struggles you may be facing today, and however pressing they may appear, remember that because you are God's child, He will shield you from the 'knock-out blows' that fly at you from all directions. That same God who took a cross and used it to become the greatest message the world has ever known, is the one who is standing at your side this very day. So go out and face your difficulties, knowing that nothing can overcome you if you belong in a personal way to Jesus.

PRAYER: Father, how can I thank You sufficiently for such a promise? I want to be a disciple who lives in the power of this thought through every minute of every day. Amen.

FOR FURTHER STUDY

2 Corinthians 12:1–10; Proverbs 2:8;
2 Timothy 4:18
1. What did God say about Paul's problem?
2. How did Paul respond?

<u>24</u> Assurance

1 JOHN 5:1–15

'I write these things to you who believe in the name of the Son of God so that you may know that you have eternal life.' (v13)

John wrote this letter in order to strengthen the disciples of Jesus in his day with the full understanding of their faith. It has special meaning for us also, right now in the twenty-first century, especially as the devil is constantly busy trying to destroy our belief in Christ and cause us to doubt the reality of our salvation. Let's equip ourselves to deal with these doubts in relation to our salvation, and see that one of the greatest ways in which we can do this is to rely entirely on the truth of God's Word.

Belonging to God

Look at the text once again: 'I write these things... that you may know that you have eternal life.' In the Bible, God has written in various ways the truth that once we have committed our lives to Him, we belong to Him for time and eternity. If we believe God's Word,

then we never need doubt the reality of our salvation. If you believe what God says, you have assurance.

'Read it for yourself!'

The story is told of a young Christian who, having accepted Jesus as his saviour, went home that night and before going to sleep read these words in his Bible: 'He who has the Son has life.' 'Thank God,' he said, 'I know I am saved because the Bible says so.' In the night, the devil came to him and said, 'You are not saved. It's all a myth.' Switching on the light, the man opened his Bible at the verse he had read before, then putting his finger on the verse, said to the devil, 'There it is – read it for yourself!'

PRAYER: Lord, help me not to listen to the devil's doubts. I see how believing his lies has caused me to lack the assurance You want me to have. Now I rest on Your Word and believe Your eternal truth. I am Yours, Lord, and You are mine, for time and for eternity. Amen.

FOR FURTHER STUDY

John 15:1–17; 2 Timothy 1:12; Hebrews 10:22
1. How do we know we are abiding in Christ's love?
2. What was Paul's assurance?

The centrepiece

JOHN 13:31–35 AND 14:21–24
'By this everyone will know that you are
my disciples, if you love one another.'
(13:35)

Here is a clear centrepiece of discipleship
– love. Men and women who don't yet
know Jesus, looking on, must sometimes
wonder what on earth we are doing.
They see our different churches, our
many denominations and our suspicion of
each other. Is it any wonder that so many
are confused and bewildered? If we really
lived the way Jesus wants us to live, then
there would be something of a revolution
in the world as people recognised this
spirit of love binding us together in a
way that no human explanation could
adequately account for.

True love

On the basis of this statement of Jesus,
we can rest assured that it is not our
teaching, talking, books, singing, music
or church attendance that is going to
cause men and women to sit up and
take notice, but a demonstration of true
love. It should not matter very much
what denomination a person belongs
to, providing they have an authentic
relationship with Jesus, but in some
circles one is not accepted unless of the
same denomination or affiliation. This is
not the way God wants us to be!

Start today

Let's decide, here and now, that with
God's help, we will endeavour to bring
home to the hearts of those outside of

the Church the importance of genuine love. We can start by first accepting all those who belong to Christ as our own brothers and sisters. Then, by refusing to allow any difference to remain – be it race, culture or politics – we can have fellowship with all God's children on the basis that, as we belong to Christ, so we belong to each other. Let's start living in a way that demonstrates we love God by loving each other.

PRAYER: Lord, I have been as guilty as others in loving only those who are part of my own circle. Help me to show the love that You talked about through every moment of my life. Amen.

FOR FURTHER STUDY
1 Corinthians 13; 1 John 3:14; 4:20
1. List the characteristics of love.
2. How will you express God's love today?

---

26 Continuing love

JOHN 15:1–16
'As the Father has loved me, so have I loved you. Now remain in my love.' (v9)

Today we are going to look at one of the reasons why many people struggle in their journey as disciples of Jesus. The Christian life is not just a life of obeying certain rules and regulations, but a loving relationship with a Saviour who died upon a cross and rose again. There are some who try to live the Christian life by looking at the commandments and attempting to live them out day by day like slaves obeying instructions. This is not the real Christian experience portrayed for us in the Bible. Christianity is not just living a good life – it goes far deeper than that: it is a loving relationship with God and His Son, Jesus.

Love and obey

If you try to serve Jesus Christ without knowing the amazing strength of His love within you, then the Christian life will soon become heavy, tiresome and boring. However, as you respond with thanks and gratitude for His love for you, which was demonstrated on the cross of Calvary, then your love for Him will enable you to live for Him day by day. It is always much easier to follow someone you love than someone you don't love. This is why Jesus talks so much about love in the New Testament. He knows you can't live for Him until you first fall in love with Him.

Every day

If you are trying to live a fruitful Christian life but are finding it difficult, talk to God about your relationship with Him. Is he the centre of your life? Ask Him to be your joy; to dethrone anything else in your life that you might have put before Him. Ask for a fresh revelation of His love every day, that you might 'remain' in it.

PRAYER: Lord Jesus, I realise that so much depends on my love for You. Please flood my whole being with that love today so that I might first love You, then live for You. In Your name I pray. Amen.

FOR FURTHER STUDY
1 John 4; John 3:16; Romans 5:8;
Ephesians 2:4–5
1. Why do we love God?
2. What does perfect love do?

27 Love as God loves

1 JOHN 4:7–21
'Dear friends, let us love one another, for love comes from God. Everyone who loves has been born of God and knows God.' (v7)

These words are just as important as the Ten Commandments, which God gave to Moses in the Old Testament. But what a joyful commandment it is! Imagine being commanded to love!

God helps you

But how can we choose to obey this commandment to love when we just don't feel like it? Well, this is where Christians find themselves in a different position from everyone else, because now that we have received Christ as our personal Saviour, God gives us a new capacity to love. You see, just as God loves everyone, even though they may seem unlovable, we can receive from Him that same ability to love as He loves. So yes, God does lift the standard very high, but He comes into our lives to help us achieve it.

God loves you

No one can love until he or she has been loved. Psychologists say that love is something we learn. If there was no love in your early childhood, you will find it difficult to love. If you received a lot of love, then loving others will come more easily to you. Nevertheless, God loves us so much that once we open ourselves to His love, then we are no longer limited by any lack of love in our childhood, and we can, therefore, go out and love in the strength of His love. Once we give ourselves to Him and allow Him to work in our lives, He will cause love for others to grow as a fruit of the Holy Spirit (Gal. 5:22). You don't have to struggle to achieve it, or even strain to express it – just be open to receive from God, and genuine love will flow from you.

PRAYER: Lord, teach me how to surrender to You this day, so that love will flow out of me to everyone. In Jesus' name. Amen.

FOR FURTHER STUDY

Ephesians 3:11–21; John 15:13; 1 John 3:16; Jeremiah 31:3

1. What kind of love does God love us with?
2. How do we become rooted in His love?

Work with enthusiasm

JOHN 5:1–19

'My Father is always at his work to this very day, and I too am working.' (v17)

The real reason for Jesus saying the words in today's Bible reading developed out of the fact that He had healed a man on the Sabbath day. The Son of God had been trying to help people understand that even though it was a day of rest, He and His Father were only too willing to break into that 'rest' to help someone who needed a miracle. God works, Jesus works, and so do we – not much can be achieved without work!

Made for work

Were you aware that work was commissioned in Scripture? Take a look at 1 Thessalonians 4:11, and you will see what I mean. We were created for purpose, and life will contain a great degree of frustration unless we are involved in good, honest work. God made our bodies for work, and our minds, temperaments and emotions are geared to this end. When work is not a part of life, there is a potential imbalance. Work, then, is to be thought of not as a task to be avoided, but as a challenge to be obeyed. We grow as we use what God has given us. So whether it is at school, college, home or your place of employment, give God your dedicated effort in everything you do.

The benefits of work

I realise, of course, that it is not always possible for people to obtain work. You might not be able to help being unemployed, but, sickness and ill health apart, you can help being without work. There is always some kind of work a healthy person can take up – helping those who are less fortunate, for example – and when it is done with enthusiasm and dignity, then it brings, not only benefit to others, but benefit to oneself as well.

PRAYER: Lord, You know how easy it is for me to take the lazy way out of things, but help me to remember Your own example, both this day and every day. Amen.

notice and care about, even though they might not seem to matter – for our characters are shaped by the sum total of the little things we find ourselves doing day by day. How much attention do you pay to the little things? If you feel that you're wasting time caring about the things that no one notices, be encouraged. Keep on faithfully serving.

Being faithful

So, are you faithful to the smaller and seemingly unimportant tasks you have to do, or impatient to get on with bigger and more impressive challenges? Jesus taught that when we are faithful in the little things, then He will be able to trust us with the bigger things. There are many Christians who are never able to do big things for God because they have never been faithful in the way they handled tasks that they perhaps considered beneath them. God is watching your life with great interest. He has great plans for you ahead – but to achieve them, remember the importance of little things. Learn to do the little things well and you will graduate to higher and greater things.

FOR FURTHER STUDY

Acts 18:1–11; 2 Thessalonians 3:10;
Romans 12:11
1. How did Paul set an example?
2. What is Paul's conclusion about not working?

29 Little things

LUKE 16:1–13

'Whoever can be trusted with very little can also be trusted with much, and whoever is dishonest with very little will also be dishonest with much.' (v10)

The story is told of a great French financier who got his start in life by picking up a pin! As a boy, he applied to a bank for a position and was refused. On the way out he stopped to pick up a pin, and as the bank manager spotted this he called him back and offered him the job. The bank manager was able to recognise that here was a boy who could handle details, and he rose to become a leading financier.

Details

The truth is that we reveal ourselves in the little things of life – the things we

PRAYER: Yes, Lord, I see that the little things are stepping-stones to greater things. I do so want to be faithful, and I ask for Your special grace to help me through these days of testing and challenge so that I might be able to do the greater things that You have prepared for me to do. Amen.

FOR FURTHER STUDY

Matthew 25:14–30; 6:33; 1 Corinthians 4:2
1. Why was the master angry with the third servant?
2. What is required of a steward?

30 Do what Jesus would do

MATTHEW 5:1–12
'Blessed are those who hunger and thirst for righteousness,
for they will be filled.' (v6)

Another important principle of successful Christian living is that whenever we are in doubt about anything, we should ask ourselves: what would Jesus do? If you ask the question in any given situation, 'What is the Christlike thing to do?' then you will not go wrong.

Breaking the moral code

It would be dangerous indeed if we were tricked into believing that we could be exempt from honouring the moral code as outlined by Jesus in the Sermon on the Mount (Matt. 5–7). However crazy it may appear to be, many great leaders have slipped into sin by rationalising the murmurs of their own self-will and believing them to be the voice of God. There is no point or purpose in trying to prevail upon God to endorse any act or attitude that is other than Christlike, for God will not go contrary to the Spirit of His Son.

Eight beautiful qualities

The principles by which Jesus lived, as outlined for us here in these eight beautiful qualities, are the principles on which the universe is built: 'Blessed are the meek... Blessed are those who hunger and thirst for righteousness... Blessed are the merciful... Blessed are the pure in heart... Blessed are the peacemakers... Blessed are those who are persecuted because of righteousness' (Matt. 5:3–10). Jesus personified these qualities and so can we. And if you think that they are above you and cannot be attained, then let me remind you again that not only does Christ lift the standard to almost unbelievable heights, but He also provides the means by which we can attain it.

PRAYER: Lord God, whenever I try to cling
to excuses, You have a way of sweeping
them from beneath my feet. I see that You
are doing this not to upset me, but to set
me up. I am grateful. Amen.

FOR FURTHER STUDY
Galatians 2:16–21; Philippians 1:21;
Matthew 10:39; 2 Corinthians 4:11
1. How can we be crucified with Christ?
2. How do we die to self?

31 The Bible

2 TIMOTHY 3:12–17

'All Scripture is God-breathed and is useful for teaching, rebuking, correcting and training in righteousness' (v16)

Having spent time considering what it means to be a follower of Jesus, we now move on to explore the topic of growing in our Christian faith. The difference between growth and stagnation in life revolves around the issue of how much time we are willing to spend with God in prayer and in the Bible.

Inspired writers

Many books have been written throughout the history of the world, but none are as important as the Bible. Some regard the Bible as a collection of old documents, seeing it as nothing more than an interesting historical record. In fact, the Bible forms one interconnected narrative – its 66 books were written by over forty different authors over a period of 1,600 years, and every writer was specially inspired by God to record what He wanted us to know.

Successful living

The main purpose of the Bible is to enable us to live successful Christian lives. Just as in the universe we discover certain laws or principles which, when obeyed, work for our benefit, so in the Scriptures we find spiritual laws or principles – signposts if you like – which enable us to stay on the road to successful living. I want to explore some of these important principles, and I assure you that if you learn them, and seek to implement them in your life and experience, they will help you grow in your faith. I believe the Bible to be the most important book in the world. Its greatest power lies in the fact that, as we read it, something happens to us. God lives in its pages and He reaches out towards us as we read.

PRAYER: Heavenly Father, my heart is
overwhelmed by the wonder of the fact that
Your power is locked up in my Bible. Unfold
Yourself to me day by day as I peruse its pages.
In Jesus' name I pray. Amen.

FOR FURTHER STUDY

Psalm 119:1–16,105; 2 Peter 1:21; Colossians 3:16

1. What did David do to avoid sin?
2. Where did the Bible come from?

Study the Scriptures

2 TIMOTHY 2:14–26

'Be a good workman, one who does not need to be ashamed when God examines your work. Know what his Word says and means.' (v15, TLB)

Today we look at the idea of a Christian being like a student. Not only are we sons and daughters in a family, soldiers in an army, athletes in an arena and sowers in a field – we are also students in a college.

The 'school of discipleship'

In the metaphorical school of discipleship, as we mentioned earlier, you will learn lessons that will stand you in good stead, not only for life but for eternity. Your textbook is the Bible. I have spoken before about the importance of reading the Bible daily, but now let me put before you the challenge of actually studying it.

Reading the Bible means reading a few verses or a passage so as to catch God's mind in the inspired words; studying the Bible means 'digging' into it, comparing one passage with another, and understanding something of the passage or chapter in relation to the verses or chapters surrounding it. To study the Bible in this sense you will need help, of course, and I want to suggest that you search out a Bible study group where the Scriptures are examined in this way. Your church leader will help you.

Explore the Bible

Don't be content just to read the Bible every day. Become involved in exploring the Word of God; find out how the Bible hangs together, and the purpose behind a particular book or passage. One thing is sure – the more you love the Bible, the more you will love God; and the more you love God, the more you will love the Bible.

PRAYER: Father, thank You for showing me the importance of studying Your precious Word. Help me to love You and Your Word, the Bible, more than I have ever done before. In Jesus' name. Amen.

FOR FURTHER STUDY

Psalm 119:89–104; Deuteronomy 11
1. What did the psalmist do during the day?
2. What does he gain from the Word of God?

Remember to meditate

JOSHUA 1:1–9

'meditate on it day and night, so that you may be careful to do everything written in it. Then you will be prosperous and successful.' (v8)

Meditation on God's Word plays a tremendous part in an effective Christian experience, and today it's important to understand that the word 'success' in the Bible is linked very closely to the word 'meditation'. That is to say, success and Bible meditation go hand in hand – you can't have one without the other. In looking at the keys to successful Christian living, we couldn't pass this one over as it is perhaps the most important of them all.

Ruminating

The truth underlying the word 'meditation' can best be illustrated in the picture of a cow chewing the cud. Once it has chewed a piece of grass, this passes into its stomach, and is then regurgitated to be chewed again and again. This happens several times until every drop of nutrition and energy is absorbed into its stomach. Something similar happens in meditation. You take a verse of Scripture and focus on it over and over again until every precious drop of truth is absorbed into your spiritual bloodstream.

Meditate on God's Word

Joshua, the great leader of the children of Israel, had one simple but vital qualification that made him successful – he knew how to meditate on the Word of God. When you take a verse of Scripture and let it lie upon your mind throughout the day and night, something tremendous happens. God's Word in your mind becomes a force that will help you have a better memory, better understanding, and enable you to grasp things in a much clearer way than ever before. So begin today to meditate on God's Word – and see the difference!

PRAYER: Lord, I am learning so many of the scriptural secrets of success. Teach me how to meditate, and help me absorb Your wonderful Word into the centre of my mind day by day. In Jesus' name. Amen.

FOR FURTHER STUDY

Psalm 1:1–6; 19:14; 63:4; 1 Timothy 4:15
1. What is promised to the man who meditates on God's Word?
2. When is a good time to meditate?

The way to greatness

MATTHEW 20:17–28

'whoever wants to become great among you must be your servant' (v26)

One of the ways, I am told, in which men are chosen as officers in the Israeli army, is by watching carefully their willingness and readiness to work under authority. They say, 'You become an officer when you have proved how you can follow another leader.'

True greatness

Israel's army policy reminds us of what Jesus said about true greatness as seen in today's text. The Living Bible translation phrases verse 27 like this: 'And if you want to be right at the top, you must serve like a slave.' Most of us want to be at the top, and perhaps we all would like to be in control of others, but God watches very carefully the way we respond to those around us before He puts us in a position of authority. When we resist and push back against authority at home or at work, or even against the civil authorities, we are, in part, resisting God (Rom. 13:1).

Authority

People's response to the authority over them will soon become the measure of their response to God. If you find it difficult to live under authority at home or work, or in any other situation, then you will have difficulty in living under the authority of your heavenly Father.

This is why, if we are to be true disciples, we must recognise the importance of this scriptural truth: that before we can ever be in a position of authority, we must first learn to work happily under authority. In the irritating, infuriating situations of your day-to-day disciplines, God is quietly working out strength, character and abilities in you, which He will one day use for His glory. But remember, to rule you must first learn to obey.

PRAYER: I see the wisdom of Your leading, heavenly Father, in first teaching me to understand the importance of authority, so that one day I might be able to supervise others well and to Your glory. Amen.

FOR FURTHER STUDY

Romans 13:1–8; Colossians 3:22–25; 1 Peter 2:17

1. How can we obey God in our daily lives?
2. How do you respond to those in authority over you?

HEBREWS 13:5–17

'Have confidence in your leaders and submit to their authority, because they keep watch over you as those who must give an account.' (v17)

One of the most important keys to living fruitful Christian lives is doing God's will. God can really do things through someone who has seen the importance of a responsive spirit. God has a wonderful plan for your life, which is unique to you, and there is no one else in the whole universe who shares that same design. Yet that plan can be frustrated and spoiled by just one thing – disobedience.

Jonah's disobedience

Jonah, an Old Testament prophet, fell into this trap. God sent him to Nineveh, where the people were engaging in outrageous sin (you can read this story for yourself in the book of Jonah). God wanted Jonah to go and preach to them, that they might change their behaviour and be spared divine judgment. But Jonah thought he knew better, and instead hopped on the first ship heading in the opposite direction. He ended up being thrown overboard in a storm, swallowed by a huge fish and later vomited onto a beach, and then headed off to Nineveh anyway! Those same circumstances most likely won't apply to us, but the lesson is there: God knows best, and His plans are worth pursuing. Let's not assume we know better.

'OK, Lord'

In other words, whatever other motive we might have for not doing what God expects, the truth is, God knows best. To obey God, and those in authority over us, is the wise and sensible thing to do. Obedience isn't a chore – if your heart is right, it will be a joy to do as God says – it is part of your worship, working out your trust in Him. God will be pleased, others will be pleased and you will enjoy it too. You are wise when you say (reverently), 'OK, Lord.'

PRAYER: Lord, I really want to follow Your guidance on this matter of obedience. Give me the strength to do it, even when I don't feel like it. In Jesus' name. Amen.

FOR FURTHER STUDY
Luke 2:41–52; Acts 5:29; Hebrews 5:8; James 1:25
1. How did Jesus demonstrate a spirit of obedience?
2. Who should we rather obey?

36 Don't worry about anything

MATTHEW 10:28-39

'So don't worry! You are more valuable to him than many sparrows.' (v31, TLB)

When the Bible tells us that we can live on this earth without worry and anxiety, it means precisely that. It is more than an academic statement – it is a concrete fact!

No need to worry!

In a youth meeting some years ago, I asked the group for a definition of a Christian. I was quite taken aback when someone said, 'A Christian is someone who has dropped the word "worry" from their vocabulary.' The Holy Spirit used that remark to show me how much time I had been wasting by worrying myself sick over something that had no basis whatsoever in reality. I took advantage of this definition to open up the whole group to a discussion on the subject: Why worry? The conclusion of that group of young people was that worry can arguably be seen as a kind of atheism. They said, 'A person who worries says, "I can't trust God, so I'll take things into my own hands."'

Worry versus faith

I thought these were pretty strong conclusions for young people under 14! Allowing for the fact that they still had most of life's troubles yet to face, the philosophy of life they were advocating was directly in line with the Scriptures. The Bible does not claim that when we follow Jesus we will not have to face any deep and serious problems, but it does claim that with God we can meet them, overcome them and assimilate them into the highest purposes of life. Worry says, 'God doesn't care, and so He won't do anything.' Faith says, 'God does care, and He and I will work it out together.' So from now on, make up your mind to listen to what faith says!

PRAYER: Lord, help me to be willing to believe Your Word, for I know that when I supply the willingness, You supply the strength. And with that combination, every day becomes a new adventure. Amen.

FOR FURTHER STUDY

Matthew 6:25-34; Philippians 4:6; 1 Peter 5:7
1. What are we to seek first?
2. Why are we not to worry?

³⁷ Learning to be humble

PHILIPPIANS 2:1–13
'he humbled himself' (v8)

Today, let's look at the one thing that can go a long way towards spoiling the peace and joy Jesus so freely gives. In one word, that thing is 'me'. Whenever anything happens, the instant reaction is, 'How will it affect *me*?' Someone else can have a catastrophe and it won't make much difference to you, but if something trivial happens in your life, then instantly it is a different matter, because the 'me' is so deeply ingrained in us all. However, if you want to know the way to fruitful Christian living, then let me explore with you, not only the things we like to know, but the things we ought to know too. We must make ourselves see that there is too much of the 'me' in our daily living. This is what so often stops us from receiving the abundant life that Jesus speaks of in His Word (John 10:10).

The unselfish life

Jesus was completely unselfish. His life was a life of prayer and love for others. Study His last hours as He is dragged through the courts in Jerusalem. As the hammer drives the nails through the sensitive network of nerves in His hands and feet, His cry is not for Himself, but for others: 'Father, forgive them, for they do not know what they are doing' (Luke 23:34).

Seek the joy of others

You have only to look at the cross to understand that this is where it all begins for you. There are many arguments that you can rally to justify the cause of 'me', but, in gazing at that bleeding and torn figure on the cross, there is only one thing you can do, and that is to turn from yourself to seek the joy of others. Jesus' mind was so centred on God that it stayed like that to the last minute of His life. Is your mind so preoccupied with yourself that you have no time for anyone but 'me'? Ask God to make your attitude like that of Jesus – humble yourself.

PRAYER: Lord, I seem far away from all that Your Word requires. Stretch out Your loving hand towards me and help me to humble myself, so that I become more like You. In Jesus' name. Amen.

FOR FURTHER STUDY
John 13:1–17; Matthew 20:28; Luke 22:27
1. How did Christ show selflessness?
2. How can we be 'servants'?

'Desert Sam'

LUKE 6:20–38
'Give, and it will be given to you. A good measure, pressed down, shaken together and running over, will be poured into your lap.' (v38)

A long time ago in the Nevada desert there stood an old well. A thirsty traveller arriving at the well saw the old pump, and started to work the mechanical contraption in the hope of getting water. But no water came! His eye fell on a piece of faded brown paper inside a rusty can on the edge of the well. Taking it out, he read these words:

The old water pump

'This pump was set up in July 1928. By the time you might need to use it the rubber washer could have worn out, and the pump will have to be primed. Under the white rock I have buried a bottle of water in which you will find exactly what you need to prime the pump. If you drink any of the water before you use it to prime the pump, then that is all the water you will get as the pump will not work. When you have done what I have said, then remember to fill up the bottle of water and leave it with this note for the next thirsty traveller. Desert Sam.'

Giving to God

Just as the old-fashioned water pumps had to have water poured into them before they would start to pump up water, so we as Christians need to put in some action of our own before our spiritual pump starts to work. This is especially true in relation to giving. Jesus said, 'Give,' (that is, you give first) 'and it will be given to you.' You see, we have to start by giving something ourselves, then God gives back to us. This is the truth of being a disciple. Put aside something for God each week or month out of what you earn. Learn to give, and you will make it possible for God to give back to you.

PRAYER: Lord, I need to learn the right way to give. Help me not to give just to get back, but show me even more clearly that giving is part of being Your disciple. Amen.

FOR FURTHER STUDY
Proverbs 3:1–10; Luke 12:41–44; 2 Corinthians 9:6–7
1. What is promised to those who give?
2. With what attitude should we give?

Giving liberally and methodically

PROVERBS 3:1-10

'Honour the LORD with your wealth, with the firstfruits of all your crops' (v9)

We have looked before at the importance of giving our money to God and His work, but today we examine the issue a little further. If giving is to become a spiritual ministry in your life, it helps to do it methodically and systematically. Don't depend on the uncertainty of feeling in relation to your giving. Decide on a more intentional and positive course of action.

Tithing

Many Christians put one-tenth of their income to one side for God week by week, or month by month, so that He has the 'first fruits' of their income. I know thousands of Christians who can tell some amazing stories of God's blessing in their lives because of this simple spiritual principle. Whatever income you receive at the moment, treat it as from God, and learn to give the first part of it to Him in some definite way. It could be done by placing

it in the offering in your church, or donating it to some missionary work. God will show you where to give it as you pray over the matter, but don't delay. Honouring God with our money is an important part of our worship.

An American millionaire by the name of Le Tourneau started out with nothing, but pledged to give one-tenth of all his income to God – and today his business is known all over the world. When we give to God, we become involved in a spiritual law that enables God to bless and prosper our lives. That prosperity is not always in financial terms. However, you can be sure that by giving to God, you open yourself to receiving from Him in a way that is beyond all telling.

PRAYER: Lord, help me to give consistently to You, because I realise that when You have first claim on everything I have, then Your blessing will flow in abundant measure. Amen.

FOR FURTHER STUDY

Malachi 3:1–12; Proverbs 11:25; 22:9
1. What had Israel done to God?
2. What did God promise if they brought their gifts to Him?

Set your affection on God

COLOSSIANS 3:1–17
'Set your minds on things above,
not on earthly things.' (v2)

Few Christians can get through their
life without finding themselves longing
for more material security. Money
commands so many things: comfort,
enjoyment, influence, power. All these
are thought to be within the reach
of those with money. Let's remind
ourselves today that if we live for no
other purpose than to accumulate
money, then our hearts will become
as metallic as the coin we seek. Too
many Christians think that a person's
life consists in the abundance of their
possessions. They have not learned that
when a bomb blasts the property they
own, or a recession reduces the value of
their savings, there are still some things
that cannot be devalued.

What belongs to others

Jesus often told the people of His day
to be on their guard against the sin of
covetousness (envying what belongs to
others): 'Do not store up for yourselves
treasures on earth, where moths and
vermin destroy, and where thieves
break in and steal' (Matt. 6:19–20).
Jesus was also careful not to dismiss
the things that add a little extra luxury
to living, but He often reminded His
hearers about the danger of 'things'
becoming master of our lives.

Materialism

How much do material things matter
to you? God has promised to supply all
our physical needs (Phil. 4:19). Beyond
this we should tread carefully, lest
the desire for the things of the world
become a snare to trap us. Enjoy the
blessings that God has given you, but
don't let them dominate your heart
to the extent that they take the place
of spiritual desire for God and His will.
Set your heart on the things that outlast
time. This is the way Jesus lived, and
we should follow His example.

**PRAYER: Make me careful, Lord,
concerning material things and their
ability to capture my heart, and give me
grace to look ever to You. Amen.**

FOR FURTHER STUDY
Luke 12:13–37; Matthew 6:19–21;
1 Timothy 6:6
1. Where should we put our treasure?
2. What was Jesus' teaching about
   possessions?

41 Keep looking to Jesus

JOHN 21:15–25

'Jesus answered, "...what is that to you? You must follow me."' (v22)

'It is none of your business!' This is what Jesus was, in effect, saying to Peter, who instead of looking at Jesus, turned around to see what John was doing, and got caught up with a matter that was simply none of his concern. Peter was looking behind at John instead of straight at Jesus. Jesus brings it to Peter's attention because He knows that so many of us get caught in the same snare.

Follow Christ

In verse 19 of this chapter, Jesus had given Peter a clear instruction: 'Follow me.' Then, only a few minutes later, Peter turns and is disturbed about John. Are you making the same mistake that Peter made – minding other people's business instead of Christ's? Perhaps another Christian has said something to upset you and you are inwardly seething and resentful? Here is one thing to learn if you are seeking to grow in your Christian experience: get your eyes off other Christians and keep them on Jesus.

Satisfaction

This does not mean, of course, that we are to ignore those Christians with whom we don't always agree, or cease to pray for them and have fellowship with them. But it does mean that we should not be too bothered about what other Christians are doing, and instead be more concerned about our own faithfulness than the faults in those who profess to serve the same Lord. One great preacher put it like this: 'When I look at you I am disappointed; when I look at myself I am disgusted. When I look at Jesus I am satisfied!'

PRAYER: Lord Jesus, help me always to look to You and not be over-concerned about the affairs of others. Speak to me again that I might hear Your Word and follow only You. In Your precious name. Amen.

FOR FURTHER STUDY
James 3; 2 Thessalonians 3:11; 1 Timothy 5:13
1. What is the most difficult part of the body to control?
2. What is God's wisdom like?

42 Be filled with the Spirit

EPHESIANS 5:8–20

'Instead, be filled with the Spirit' (v18)

In Christian circles we often refer to God as a 'Trinity'. We use this word to describe the truth that God, though one, consists of three separate persons: Father, Son and Holy Spirit. That God can be one, yet three in one, is indeed a great mystery. Don't try to puzzle it out – it will become clearer to you each day as you grow in your Christian life and experience. It is important to see, however, that when you became a Christian, each member of the Trinity was involved in your coming to faith.

God, the Father, forgave you; Christ, the Son, brought to your heart the amazing assurance that you are forgiven; and the Holy Spirit was the one who produced in your life the miracle of the new birth.

The Holy Spirit's work

The work of the Holy Spirit in enabling you to live a positive and dynamic Christian life is far greater than you probably realise. He reveals more about Jesus to you through God's Word, the Bible, and He supplies the strength by which you can be the kind of Christian God wants you to be. Let's seek to be constantly filled with the Holy Spirit so that our life overflows with God's love and power.

Every area of your life

The Holy Spirit has already been at work in your life from the time you first accepted Jesus until now. But He longs to fill not just a part, but the whole of your being. All Christians have the Holy Spirit but the Holy Spirit doesn't have all Christians. By that I mean that every follower of Jesus has some experience of the Holy Spirit working within them, but there are parts of the personality to which He has not been given access. Ask God right now to fill every part of your being with His Spirit, so that every area of your life is brought under His influence. Then continue to keep your life open to the Spirit every day so that you have a constant experience of His filling and empowering.

PRAYER: Dear Lord, please fill me with Your Spirit today, and take over every part of my life, so that I can be a bold and effective witness for Jesus Christ. In Jesus' name I pray. Amen.

FOR FURTHER STUDY
Acts 10:34–48; Galatians 5:22–23; Romans 8:14; 2 Corinthians 3:6
1. What happened when Peter preached?
2. List the Holy Spirit's fruit in your life.

Discover your basic gift

ROMANS 12:3–8
'We have different gifts, according to the grace given to each of us.' (v6)

Some young Christians might say, 'I'm not gifted to speak, sing or do anything for the Lord. What use am I to Him?' Well, I have news for you! Every Christian is gifted by God to do at least one thing well for Him. In other words, there is something you can do for God that no one else could do as effectively as you. I can't tell you what that something is, but you can discover it for yourself. Here's how.

Part of the body

Think of the Church of Jesus Christ as Paul describes it here – as a body. Then reflect on how important every part of the body is to the other parts. Can the heart do without the lungs or can the eye do without the finger? (Especially when grit gets into it!) Each part is sensitive to the needs of the other parts, and God has put within you a sensitivity to help meet the needs of other Christians. Once you discover what you are most sensitive to, then you can begin to contribute along that line to the health of the 'body', which is the Church.

We can contribute

The Bible lists seven ways in which we can contribute to the Church: preaching, serving, teaching, stimulating or encouraging the faith of others, giving, leadership, and sympathy. God has designed you to build His Church in at least one of these seven ways. He may develop you into a preacher, a teacher, a server, a counsellor, a giver, a leader or someone with deep sympathy for others. In the days ahead, ask God to show you just where you fit into the 'body', and to give you His own special witness in your heart as to exactly what gift He has given you.

PRAYER: Lord, there is enough food for thought here to last me a lifetime. Show me clearly what function You mean me to have in Your Church, so that I might be able to be the person You want me to be. In Jesus' name. Amen.

FOR FURTHER STUDY
1 Corinthians 12:11–31;
Ephesians 1:23; 4:11–16
1. To what does Paul liken the Church?
2. How does this work?

A living memorial

LUKE 22:7–20

'And he took bread, gave thanks and broke it, and gave it to them, saying, "This is my body given for you; do this in remembrance of me."' (v19)

Throughout time mankind has endeavoured to be remembered. To keep from being forgotten, we erect monuments, write books, endow large gifts, build hospitals, schools etc.

A meaningful meal

Think how Jesus must have felt at what the Church calls The Last Supper. Surrounded by His 12 disciples, in the very shadow of the cross, Jesus wanted to help us remember. With clear understanding and knowing of man's tendency to forget, Jesus instituted this simple but meaningful meal of bread and wine. This meal has been described by someone as a living memorial as it points, of course, to the living Jesus, who once died but is now alive forever!

Remembering Christ

He asked us to remember Him in this special way as often as possible, and in order to be a growing disciple of Jesus, it's helpful for you to share in this simple meal as often as you can. Whatever your age, I encourage you to be present at the times when your church celebrates the Lord's Supper. Some denominations call it the Eucharist or Holy Communion, while some refer to it simply as the Breaking of Bread. Much of it may not

be clear, but enter into it in this spirit: that you need to experience it because it speaks of Jesus, and because you long to know more of Him. The broken bread speaks of His broken body. The red wine speaks of His blood that was shed for your sin. As you see them, you are reminded vividly of His love.

PRAYER: Blessed Jesus, how glad I am that You have left this living memorial for me to be reminded of Your undying love. Help me to enter into the real meaning of it in a new way from this day forward. Amen.

FOR FURTHER STUDY

1 Corinthians 11:23–32; 10:16;
Hebrews 10:19–23
1. What are we to do before taking Holy Communion?
2. How often do you take Holy Communion?

Fan the flames

HEBREWS 10:12–25

'let us consider how we may spur one another on towards love and good deeds, not giving up meeting together' (vv24–25)

'Going to church,' says Dr Billy Graham, 'doesn't make a person a Christian any more than going to a garage makes him

a motorcar.' We can see the point of this observation, of course, but once a person becomes a Christian, they grow and flourish in the relationships and encouragement that comes from being with other believers, in order to keep active and alert. The Church exists to glorify God, but it is also for our benefit!

Going to church

A young Christian said to his minister one day, 'But I don't need to come regularly to church in order to be a good Christian.' The minister said nothing, but reached over to the fireplace and picked out a red-hot piece of coal, then left it on one side to cool. After a few minutes the red-hot coal lost its glow, and the minister turned to the young man with this remark: 'Just as that piece of coal lost its glow when taken out of the fire, so will you lose your glow if you think you can do without the Church.' God's pattern for Christians in general is that we meet together as often as possible – we are strengthened when we share life together in community.

Christian fellowship

It is hard to explain what happens when believers meet in Jesus' name to sing, worship and pray; but throughout the past two thousand years the Church of Jesus Christ has derived miraculous strength and supernatural energy from such gatherings. To be true disciples, let's not ignore the strength and power that comes from meeting as often as possible in Jesus' name. Meeting with our brothers and sisters in Christian fellowship is a distinct and unique experience, greater than anything in any other part of society.

PRAYER: Thank You, Father, for showing me today the importance of fellowship with other believers. How glad I am that I am a member of the body of Christ. Help me to develop close, loving relationships with other believers. In Jesus' name. Amen.

FOR FURTHER STUDY
Acts 12:1–19; Psalm 84:4; 133:1–3
1. How did God answer the Early Church's prayers for Peter?
2. Where does God command His blessing?

HEBREWS 13:12–21

'With Jesus' help we will continually offer our sacrifice of praise to God by telling others of the glory of his name.' (v15, TLB)

Some Christians, when overtaken by difficulties and trials, may quickly assume that God has deserted them. They might interpret storms in life as evidence that God has withdrawn His presence. Nothing, of course, could be further from the truth. In all of life's problems, God is always there – caring, concerned and compassionate. The fact that difficulties crowd in upon us should not be taken as proof that He does not care. He has promised: 'I will never, *never* fail you nor forsake you' (Heb. 13:5, TLB).

A venture of faith

As we grow in our faith we begin to realise that in every trouble or trial, God never deserts those who are His, and they find it possible to praise Him even when it feels as if they have been abandoned. Praise at such a time may well be called a 'sacrifice', as it is a willingness to pour out thanksgiving when all around is black and foreboding and God seems far away. In the long run, life works best when we reach out in an adoring venture of faith to praise God with daring defiance, even though reason rises up and argues to the contrary. The leap of praise that rises from hearts that are crushed and almost broken must be a wonder to angels, and a constant delight to the heart of God.

Praise God anyway

You may not feel like praising God in the midst of your difficulties, but go ahead and praise Him anyway – and watch the results! Don't wilt when life is looking bleak, but prompt your heart and voice to express sincere, meaningful, powerful praise. Such sacrifice is precious in His sight.

PRAYER: Lord, in the face of all that threatens to dampen my heart today, I lift my voice in sincere praise and adoration of Your name. I praise You that all things are working for my good and for Your glory. Amen.

FOR FURTHER STUDY

Luke 19:29–40; Psalm 100:4; 107:22; Colossians 3:15

1. How did Jesus answer the Pharisees?
2. List what you can praise God for today.

Jesus Christ is Lord

PHILIPPIANS 2:4–11

'at the name of Jesus every knee should bow... and every tongue acknowledge that Jesus Christ is Lord' (vv10-11)

One of the most amazing truths of Scripture is that – Jesus Christ is Lord and because of this, He has the last word in everything. It may seem a naive thing to say now, surrounded by poverty and injustice as we are, but it is nevertheless true, that the man who walked the dusty roads of Palestine and died on a cross is now upon the throne of the universe and will have the last word in human affairs. I know to some this may sound crazy. Yet for those who have eyes to see, human affairs are working out just that way. Everything that is in harmony with the will of God survives, but everything that is against that will perishes. There's not much sign of that at the moment, you may think, but believe me, the day is coming when the temporal will be swept away and only that which is eternal will remain.

The A–Z

Jesus Christ is the only rock on which life can be established, and if life is not built upon Him then it will ultimately perish. He is the alpha and the omega (Rev. 1:8). As the alpha (the first letter of the Greek alphabet), He is the beginning, and as the omega (the last letter of the Greek alphabet), He is the end. Jesus has the first and final word in the construction and in the maintenance of the universe: 'He is before all things, and in him all things hold together' (Col. 1:17). Despite all the apparent evidence to the contrary, He will bring all things to a satisfactory and final conclusion.

An optimist

The reason I am an optimist in the midst of the present situation is because I have read the last chapters of the book of Revelation. In those chapters, Jesus is revealed as the conqueror of sin, death and hell. So we carry with us into the future this one sustaining thought: as we crown Christ Lord of all – we win!

PRAYER: Lord Jesus Christ, my heart is Yours, my mind is Yours, my whole being is Yours. You are my King, my creator, and my everlasting Lord. Amen.

FOR FURTHER STUDY

Acts 2:14–36; Revelation 5:6–14; 7:9–12; John 1:29; 1 Corinthians 8:6
1. What did Peter declare?
2. What are the attributes of the Lamb of God?

2 CORINTHIANS 3:1–11
'Such confidence we have through Christ before God.' (v4)

It is surprising how many Christians trust Jesus to save them from their sins, but then don't seem to want to involve Him more deeply in their lives. We get to know Jesus in a similar way as we would get to know anyone else around us; we strike up an acquaintance with someone, we listen to what they have to say, we learn to trust them, and on that raft of trust we launch out deeper and deeper into the realm of closer personal relationship.

Trusting Christ

Someone put it like this: 'We get to know Christ more deeply in the same way that we learn to swim. No one ever learned to swim by theory alone. After it has all been explained and demonstrated, the time comes to get into the water, and trust yourself to its supporting power. There is no other way to swim.' So it is with your Christian experience. Reading the Bible is one thing – do you trust what it says? Knowing Jesus can take care of every area of your life is one thing – but do you trust Him to actually do it? It involves

giving and taking – an experiment of trusting Him on one part of His Word before moving out on to another.

From sinner to saint

You are not the first person to 'experiment' in this way. For two thousand years, Jesus has been coming into the lives of men and women and transforming them. So you are invited to trust! Start to trust Him a little at first (new swimmers usually go in at the shallow end), and then trust Him more as the days go by. Trust Him to answer that prayer, to work out that difficulty, to help you manage that temper. The speed with which He takes over full control depends very much on your willingness to trust Him in all He says He can do.

PRAYER: Lord, teach me the trust of a childlike faith that accepts Your Word as final, and believes in all You are planning for me. In Jesus' name. Amen.

FOR FURTHER STUDY
1 Samuel 17; Psalm 37:5; 118:8; Isaiah 26:3
1. Where was David's trust?
2. What did David say to his enemy?

See yourself as a child of God

ROMANS 8:1–17
The Spirit himself testifies with our spirit that we are God's children.' (v16)

There are two pitfalls to be aware of in our Christian life. One is the abyss of pride; the other is the pit of inferiority. No Christian should pander to pride, and no Christian should feel inferior. Now I know I am in danger of being misunderstood, but hold steady for a moment and you will see what I mean. Let's not confuse inferiority with humility. An inferiority complex is a damaging thing. Though it normally develops in youth, it can often stay with you right throughout your life.

Don't despise yourself
Some Christian writers confuse humility and inferiority, and encourage people to despise themselves. This is not the Bible's teaching. No one is to be despised, even by themselves, when they are so dear to God that He shed His precious blood for them. This, in itself, causes us to stop and pause and reconsider. God does not love us because we are good and clever; He loves us for ourselves alone. Once your sins are forgiven, you are a child of God. You are the son or daughter of a King! People called Jesus a carpenter, and indeed He was – but watch Him stride through the New Testament. He brings a dignity and a poise to every page of the Gospels as He moves through life with the consciousness that He is the Son of God.

Pride and inferiority
You might be thinking, 'Well, that was OK for Jesus because He was the Son of God!' But we too are sons and daughters of the living God. This truth, when allowed to sink deep into our spirits, can help us to throw back our shoulders and begin to walk through life with the dignity and bearing of the child of the King. How can any child of God feel inferior? We are not to feel proud, but are not to feel inferior either. We are saved from the abyss of pride because we are bought by His blood. We are saved from the pit of inferiority because He has made us His sons and daughters.

PRAYER: Lord, root out every trace of inferiority in my soul and make me gloriously aware that I am a child of the King. In Jesus' name. Amen.

FOR FURTHER STUDY
Luke 14:1–11; Philippians 4:11–13; Proverbs 16:19; 29:23
1. What did Jesus teach about humility?
2. How did Paul deal with his different circumstances?

God has not finished with you

JOHN 1:35–42

'Jesus looked intently at Peter... and then said, "You are Simon, John's son
– but you shall be called Peter, the rock!"' (v42, TLB)

The transition between what we are and what we can be is outworked by Jesus Christ, and by Him alone. When Jesus looked at Simon Peter, He saw a reed blown about by the wind. But Jesus sees with a dual vision. He saw him not only as he was (a reed), but as he could be (a rock). Grace flowing through this temperamental disciple changed him into a person of strong and solid convictions.

Take heart

As you have gone through the daily readings in this special issue of *Every Day with Jesus*, you may have felt that you are still far from the person God wants you to be. But, take heart! God has not finished with you yet. Moment by moment, with infinite patience and skill, God is working through your life to bring it to the perfection for which He longs. I particularly appreciate The Living Bible's wonderful translation of Romans 8:29, 'For from the very beginning God decided that those who came to him—and all along he knew who would—should become like his Son'. All God's love and grace is working now to transform us into the people He wants us to be. Given our consent and co-operation, that end can be achieved to a great measure this very day.

Let go – let God

Cast your mind back over the challenge of these readings. Reflect upon the daily discussion you have had with Jesus. How have you been drawn closer to Him? How have you longed to be more like Him? That longing will not be overlooked, for He who sees your innermost heart knows your strivings, your longings and aspirations. The change will come by letting go – and letting God. Don't struggle, don't fight, don't strive. Just rest in Him. Let Him work the miracle. All you can do is to fill the water jars with water – He will turn the water into wine!

PRAYER: Lord, today I give myself fully into Your hands. Make me more like Jesus than I have ever been before. This I pray in Your name. Amen.

FOR FURTHER STUDY
2 Timothy 2; Philippians 1:6; Isaiah 40:31;
2 Corinthians 4:16; 1 Timothy 1:12
1. What was Paul's persuasion?
2. About what was he confident?

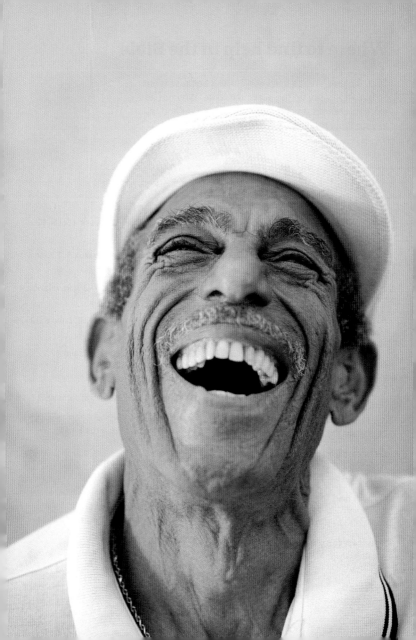

Where to find help in the Bible

Each Bible reference has been chosen because it has something to say on the particular issue. Why not add extra references on different subjects as you find them in your Bible readings.

Addicted
Mark 5:1–20; John 8:32; Galatians 5:19–23

Alone
Esther 4; Psalm 68:1–10; John 14:15–21

Angry
Ephesians 4:25–32; John 2:12–22;
James 1:19–20

Anxious
Matthew 6:25–34; John 14:1–4;
Philippians 4:19

Bereaved
Mark 14:12–26; 1 Corinthians 15:50–55;
1 Thessalonians 4:13–18

Concern for surroundings
Genesis 2:15–17; Psalm 8:1–9;
Colossians 1:15–20

Concern for justice
Jeremiah 2:34–35; Amos 8:4–8;
Luke 3:1–18

Concerned for suffering
Nehemiah 5:1–11; Psalm 82;
Mark 14:32–35

Concern for world peace
Isaiah 11:1–9; Matthew 24:4–6;
Romans 13:1–7

Defeated
Psalm 60; Isaiah 53; 2 Timothy 4:1–8

Depressed
Job 7:1–8; Psalm 30; Luke 15:11–32

Discouraged
Numbers 21:4–9; Habbakuk 3; 1 John 5:1–15

Excited
Psalm 118; Luke 10:17–20; Revelation 4

Fearful
Psalm 27; 1 Kings 19:1–18; Luke 8:22–25

Full of praise
Deuteronomy 8:10–18; Psalm 47;
Ephesians 5:15–20

Ill
2 Kings 5:1–14; Psalm 38; James 5:17–18

Impatient
Exodus 17:1–7; Proverbs 19:11;
Colossians 1:9–14

Lacking confidence
Judges 6:11–24; Isaiah 7:9;
Matthew 14:22–23

Lacking faith
2 Kings 7; Psalm 130; Mark 9:23–24

Needing advice
Exodus 18:13–26; 1 Samuel 23:1–5;
James 1:7–9

Needing courage
Joshua 1:1–9; Psalm 76; Acts 2:1–13

Needing God
2 Samuel 1; Psalm 28; Habbakuk 1:1-4

Needing love
Psalm 103; Isaiah 66:10-14; Romans 5:8

Needing persistence
Mark 10:46-52; Isaiah 35:1-10;
Hebrews 10:32-39

Pressured
Mark 15:1-20; Proverbs 1:10-19;
Romans 12:1-2; Matthew 11:28-30

Rejected
Psalm 139; 2 Corinthians 11:1-11;
2 Timothy 4:16-18

Rescued
Exodus 15; Psalm 30; Jonah 2:2-9

Sad
1 Samuel 1; 2 Corinthians 1:3-11;
Revelation 21:1-5

Scared of death
Job 19:25-27; Luke 23:39-43;
Acts 7:54-60

Short of money
Exodus 16:2-15; Luke 12:22-31;
James 4:13-15

Sinful
Numbers 21:4-9; Luke 18:9-14;
Romans 8:1-13

Sorry
Psalm 51; Luke 15:11-24; 1 John 1:9

Tempted
Psalm 119:9; 1 Corinthians 10:13

Threatened
1 Samuel 19; Ezekiel 2:4-9; Mark 13:9-11

Tired
1 Kings 19:1-6; Isaiah 40:31

Too old
Psalm 71; Joel 2:28-29; 1 Timothy 5:1-10

Too young
1 Samuel 3; Jeremiah 1:6-10;
1 Timothy 4:12

Unable to cope
Genesis 21:8-15; Psalm 116;
2 Corinthians 11:16-30

Wanting to pray
Daniel 9; Matthew 6:5-15; Acts 4:23-31

Weak
Exodus 19:4; Joel 3:9-11;
2 Corinthians 12:7-10

This table of references has been taken from the New Century Version (Anglicised Edition) Bible.

Copyright © 1993 by Nelson Word Ltd, 9 Holden Ave, Bletchley, Milton Keynes. MK1 1QR, UK. Used with permission.

Continue your journey.
Every day.

If you have been encouraged and inspired by this booklet, you can continue spending time with God every day using our daily Bible reading notes – there's something for everyone...

Every Day with Jesus
Selwyn Hughes' renowned writing is updated by Mick Brooks into these trusted and popular notes.

Inspiring Women Every Day
Encouragement, uplifting scriptures and insightful daily thoughts for women.

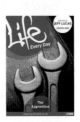

Life Every Day
Jeff Lucas helps apply the Bible to daily life through his trademark humour and insight.

The Manual
Straight-talking guides to help men walk daily with God. Written by Carl Beech.

To find out more about all our daily Bible reading notes, or to take out a subscription, visit **cwr.org.uk/biblenotes** or call 01252 784700. Also available in Christian bookshops.

 Printed format   Large print format   Email format   Ebook format